TABLE OF CONTENTS

A Crabtree Seedlings Book

School-to-Home Support for Caregivers and Teachers

This book helps children grow by letting them practice reading. Here are a few guiding questions to help the reader build his or her comprehension skills. Possible answers appear in red.

Before Reading:

- What do I know about Georgia?
    - *I know that Georgia is a state.*
    - *I know that Georgia grows peaches.*
- What do I want to learn about Georgia?
    - *I want to learn which famous people were born in Georgia.*
    - *I want to learn what the state flag looks like.*

During Reading:

- What have I learned so far?
    - *I have learned that Atlanta is the state capital of Georgia.*
    - *I have learned that there are dolphins at Driftwood Beach.*
- I wonder why...
    - *I wonder why the state flower is the Cherokee rose.*
    - *I wonder why the Toaccoa River is good for tubing.*

After Reading:

- What did I learn about Georgia?
    - *I have learned that Cumberland Island has beaches.*
    - *I have learned that the state animal is the white-tailed deer.*
- Read the book again and look for the glossary words.
    - *I see the word **capital** on page 6, and the word **cobbler** on page 10. The other glossary words are found on pages 22 and 23.*

GEORGIA
Hi! My name is Shumari. Welcome to Georgia!

I live in Savannah. There are many old, pretty, brick buildings in Savannah.

My city has a lot of **squares**.

Georgia is in the southeastern United States. The **capital** is Atlanta.

Fun Fact: Atlanta is the largest city in Georgia.

The state animal is the white-tailed deer.

The Cherokee rose is the state flower.

We grow a lot of peaches. Some of them are used to make my favorite dessert, peach **cobbler**.

Fun Fact: Georgia has 1.6 million peach trees.

My state flag has red and white stripes. The state **seal** is on the left.

There are three national sports teams in Georgia.

I like to visit Driftwood Beach on Jekyll Island. Sometimes we see dolphins.

Fun Fact: More than 50 kinds of animals live on Jekyll Island.

I can see many sea animals at Georgia Aquarium.

I like to ride the roller coasters with my family at Six Flags Over Georgia.

Civil rights leader Martin Luther King Jr. was born in Georgia. Baseball player Jackie Robinson was also born in Georgia.

Fun Fact: President Jimmy Carter was born in Plains, Georgia.

My favorite beach is at Cumberland Island.

It is exciting to go **tubing** on the Toccoa River.

Glossary

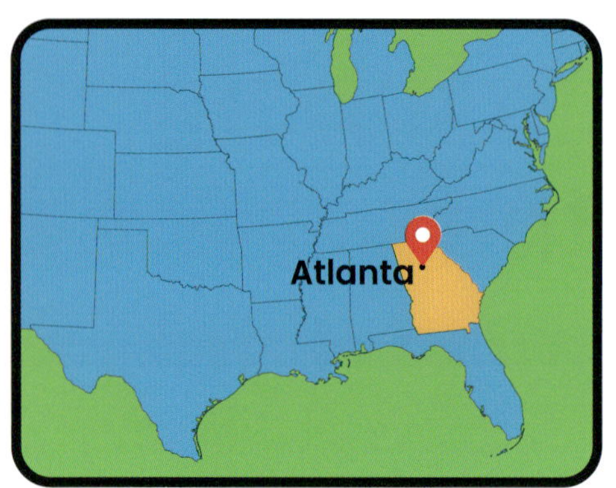

capital (cap-ih-tuhl): The city or town where the government of a country, state, or province is located

civil rights (siv-uhl rahyts): The rights every person should have in their country

cobbler (kob-ler): A dessert made of cooked fruit covered with a thick crust

seal (seel): A special design that is used on important papers and other items

squares (skwairz): Open public areas where people gather

tubing (too-bing): Riding down a river on an inner tube

Index

About the Author

Christina Earley lives in sunny South Florida with her husband and son. She enjoys traveling around the United States and learning about different historical places. Her hobbies include hiking, yoga, and baking.

Written by: Christina Earley
Designed and Illustrated by: Bobbie Houser
Series Development: James Earley
Proofreader: Melissa Boyce
Educational Consultant: Marie Lemke M.Ed.

Photographs:
Alamy: Alpha Historica: p. 18 left, 22; IanDagnall Computing: p. 19 right; GL Archive: p. 19
Shutterstock: Sean Pavone: cover, 3, 4; William Silver: p. 5, 23; Volina: p. 6, 22; f11photo: p. 7; Tom Reichner: p. 8; Paul Brennan: p. 9; Maria Dryfhout: p. 10-11, 22; Nyura: p. 11; railway fx: p. 12, 23; Jamie Lamor Thompson: p. 13; Kevin Ruck: p. 14-15; Steve Samples: p. 15; Photo Rebel: p. 16; Paul Brennan: p. 17; Josiah True: p. 20; Kelly vanDellen: p. 21, 23

Crabtree Publishing

crabtreebooks.com 800-387-7650

Printed in the U.S.A./012023/CG20220815

Published in Canada
Crabtree Publishing
616 Welland Avenue
St. Catharines, Ontario
L2M 5V6

Published in the United States
Crabtree Publishing
347 Fifth Avenue
Suite 1402-145
New York, New York, 10016

Library and Archives Canada Cataloguing in Publication
Available at Library and Archives Canada

Library of Congress Cataloging-in-Publication Data
Available at the Library of Congress

Hardcover: 978-1-0396-9653-2
Paperback: 978-1-0396-9760-7
Ebook (pdf): 978-1-0396-9974-8
Epub: 978-1-0396-9867-3